W9-BMB-804

★ IT'S MY STATE! ★

INDIANA

Kathleen Derzipilski

Richard Hantula

Marshall Cavendish
Benchmark
New York

Published by Marshall Cavendish Benchmark
An imprint of Marshall Cavendish Corporation

Website: www.marshallcavendish.us

Other Marshall Cavendish Offices:
Marshall Cavendish International (Asia) Private Limited, 1 New Industrial Road, Singapore 536196 • Marshall Cavendish International (Thailand) Co Ltd. 253 Asoke, 12th Flr, Sukhumvit 21 Road, Klongtoey Nua, Wattana, Bangkok 10110, Thailand • Marshall Cavendish (Malaysia) Sdn Bhd, Times Subang, Lot 46, Subang Hi-Tech Industrial Park, Batu Tiga, 40000 Shah Alam, Selangor Darul Ehsan, Malaysia

Marshall Cavendish is a trademark of Times Publishing Limited

All websites were available and accurate when this book was sent to press.

Library of Congress Cataloging-in-Publication Data
Derzipilski, Kathleen.
        Indiana / Kathleen Derzipilski and Richard Hantula.—2nd ed.
            p. cm. — (It's my state!)
        Summary: "Surveys the history, geography, government, economy, and people
        of Indiana"—Provided by publisher.
        Includes bibliographical references and index.
        ISBN 978-1-60870-522-1 (print) — ISBN 978-1-60870-700-3 (ebook)
        1. Indiana—Juvenile literature. I. Hantula, Richard. II. Title. III.
        Series.
    F526.3.D47 2012
    977.2—dc22   2010044333

Second Edition developed for Marshall Cavendish Benchmark by RJF Publishing LLC (www.RJFpublishing.com)
Series Designer, Second Edition: Tammy West/Westgraphix LLC

All maps, illustrations, and graphics © Marshall Cavendish Corporation. Maps and artwork on pages 6, 28, 29, 75 (top), 76, and back cover by Christopher Santoro. Map and graphics on pages 9 and 43 by Westgraphix LLC.

The photographs in this book are used by permission and through the courtesy of:
Front cover: Richard Cummins/Alamy and IIene MacDonald/Alamy (inset).
Alamy: Arco Images GmbH, 4 (top), 19; Daniel Dempster Photography, 4 (bottom), 10 (top), 66, 70; CR Photography, 5; Jim West, 8; Alexey Stiop, 10 (bottom), 62, 73; Don Smetzer, 12, 27; www.rwongphoto.com, 13, 14; Richard Oliver, 15; Chris Howes/Wild Places, 16; Steve Apps, 17; Fred LaBounty, 18 (right); Jeff Greenberg, 20, 44, 45; North Wind Picture Archives, 22, 25; Ivy Close Images, 35; David R. Frazier Photolibrary, Inc., 52; Nick Suydam, 60; Ingram Publishing, 63; Steve Cavalier, 68; ccMacroshots, 69 (left); Mike Briner, 72; Tom Uhlman, 74. **Associated Press:** 18 (left), 31, 36, 38, 43, 48, 51, 58. **Cook Medical Inc:** 49, Courtesy of Cook Medical Inc. **Getty Images:** NBAE, 40; Getty Images, 46, 47 (top); FilmMagic, 47 (bottom); WireImage, 50. **Superstock:** Richard Cummins, 21, 75 (bottom); Superstock, 34; William Strode, 42; age fotostock, 56; Medical RF, 69 (right). **The Image Works:** Jeff Greenberg, 64.

Printed in Malaysia (T).
135642

CONTENTS

A Quick Look at Indiana 4

1 The Hoosier State 7
    Indiana Counties Map 9
    Plants & Animals 18

2 From the Beginning 21
    Making Potpourri 28
    Important Dates 39

3 The People 41
    Who Indianans Are 43
    Famous Indianans 46
    Calendar of Events 50

4 How the Government Works 53
    Branches of Government 55

5 Making a Living 61
    Recipe for Mint-Chocolate Brownies 63
    Workers & Industries 65
    Products & Resources 68

State Flag & Seal 75
Indiana State Map 76
State Song 77
More About Indiana 78
Index 79

State Tree: Tulip Tree

The tulip tree is among the tallest trees in Indiana's forests. The tree has clusters of bell-shaped flowers. The distinctive leaves of the tulip tree appear on the Indiana state seal. The tulip tree is also sometimes called the yellow poplar.

State Flower: Peony

The peony was chosen as the state flower in 1957. In the spring, the plants produce large, fragrant flowers in shades of white, pink, and red. Because of their beautiful flowers and dark green, glossy leaves, peonies are grown in gardens and yards throughout Indiana.

State Bird: Cardinal

The cardinal can be found in Indiana throughout the year. The male cardinal is easily identified by its bright red feathers and crest (the feathers that form a point at the top of its head). The female has brown feathers and a light red head and crest. Cardinals flit through shrubs, thickets, and trees. They eat a variety of insects, seeds, and small fruits.

State Stone: Salem Limestone

Indiana limestone originated more than 300 million years ago when the Midwest was under an inland sea. The limestone was formed from layers of microscopic fossils of the animals that once lived in that sea. The beautiful, fine-textured stone is taken from quarries in central and southern Indiana. Indiana limestone has been used in many buildings throughout the country, including structures in New York City and Washington, D.C.

State River: Wabash River

The Wabash River and its valley have long attracted settlers and explorers. Many American Indian towns and camps were located along the Wabash. The French established trading posts and forts on the riverbanks. For early white settlers, the Wabash was a trade route for farm products and other goods. The river's name comes from the Miami Indian word *Wah-Ba-Shi-Ki*, which means "pure white." This probably referred to the limestone over which the river flows in its upper sections.

State Language: English

Indiana adopted English as the official language of the state in 1984. In Indiana—as in all the other states— government meetings are conducted in English, and official records and legal documents are written in English. In 1995, Indiana also gave official recognition to American Sign Language, the chief sign language used by deaf Americans.

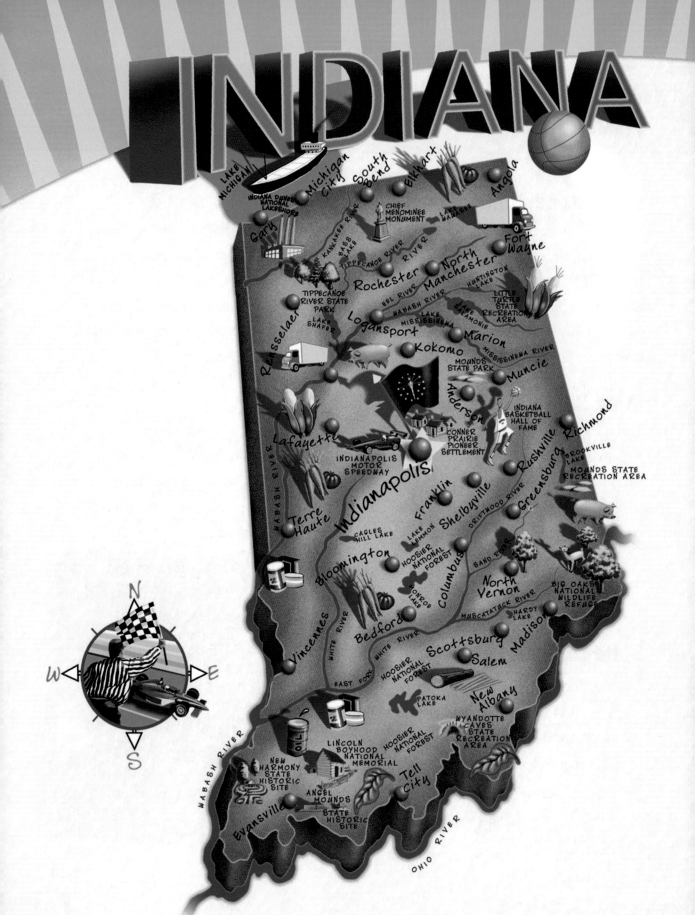

INDIANA

Lake Michigan
Michigan City
South Bend
Elkhart
Angola
Indiana Dunes National Lakeshore
Gary
Kankakee River
Chief Menominee Monument
Lake Wawasee
Fort Wayne
Babb Lake
Tippecanoe River
Eel River
Rochester
North Manchester
Huntington Lake
Little Turtle State Recreation Area
Tippecanoe River State Park
Wabash River
Logansport
Lake Salamonie
Lake Shafer
Lake Mississinewa
Marion
Mississinewa River
Rensselaer
Kokomo
Mounds State Park
Muncie
Lafayette
Anderson
Indiana Basketball Hall of Fame
Richmond
Conner Prairie Pioneer Settlement
Rushville
Greensburg
Brookville Lake
Indianapolis Motor Speedway
Mounds State Recreation Area
Wabash River
Terre Haute
Indianapolis
Franklin
Shelbyville
Driftwood River
Greensburg
Eagles Hill Lake
Lake Lemmon
Sand Creek
Bloomington
Hoosier National Forest
Columbus
North Vernon
Big Oaks National Wildlife Refuge
Vincennes
Monroe Lake
Muscatatuck River
Hardy Lake
White River
Bedford
White River
Scottsburg
Madison
East Fork
Hoosier National Forest
Salem
Patoka Lake
New Albany
OIL
Lincoln Boyhood National Memorial
Hoosier National Forest
Wyandotte Caves State Recreation Area
Wabash River
New Harmony State Historic Site
Angel Mounds State Historic Site
Tell City
Evansville
Ohio River

N
W E
S

The Hoosier State

Indiana is located in the north-central part of the United States. Roughly rectangular in shape, Indiana is bounded on the south by the Ohio River. Its northwest corner touches Lake Michigan, one of the Great Lakes. Indiana has a land area of 35,867 square miles (92,895 square kilometers). In size, it is the thirty-eighth largest state. It is divided into ninety-two counties.

Land Shaped by Glaciers and an Ancient Sea

More than 300 million years ago, much of North America was under water. Over the past one million years, the northern part of the continent has experienced several periods when glaciers—large, slow-moving ice masses—formed and traveled over the land. As the glaciers moved, they shaped the land. Then, as the climate warmed, these masses of ice melted and retreated northward. Scientists think that the land that now includes Indiana has been under glaciers a number of times in the past million years. Evidence of the ancient sea and the glaciers is visible in the geography of Indiana.

The movement of the glaciers left most of Indiana flat or rolling and covered with

Quick Facts

INDIANA BORDERS

North	Michigan
	Lake Michigan
South	Kentucky
East	Ohio
West	Illinois

Glaciers moving across the region thousands of years ago helped create the dunes that line Indiana's Lake Michigan shoreline.

sandy, fertile soil called till. The pockets of marshes and ponds in the northern part of the state are another sign of the thawing glaciers. The glaciers carved up the land and left water behind. The sand dunes along the shores of Lake Michigan are made up of windblown debris that was created by past glaciers. As each glacier formed and then melted, it reshaped the region's rivers and the shoreline of Lake Michigan.

Southern Indiana was largely untouched by the glaciers, but it was affected by the great inland sea. While the land was under water, layers of limestone and dolomite—a type of mineral—were laid down. These stones were easily dissolved and eroded by underground streams. The result is the hilly surface and the knobs, ravines,

DUNE DIVERSITY

Quick Facts

The sand dunes in the Indiana Dunes National Lakeshore on Lake Michigan rise to a height of nearly 200 feet (60 meters). The national lakeshore, which covers about 15,000 acres (6,000 hectares), contains not only dunes but also oak grassland, swamps, marshes, prairies, rivers, forests, and beaches. In terms of number of species per acre, it features one of the most diverse collections of plants of any site managed by the U.S. National Park Service. These species range from grasses to tall white pines to algae. More than 1,100 types of flowering plants and ferns live there.

Indiana Counties

Indiana has 92 counties.

Underground caves are common in southern Indiana. Squire Boone Caverns is a popular site for visitors.

bluffs, and sinkholes found in southern Indiana. Streams disappear into the ground or emerge as springs. Many caves can be found underground. This type of landscape is called karst.

Forests and Prairies

Most of Indiana's trees are deciduous hardwoods such as maple, elm, ash, beech, hickory, oak, cherry, walnut, and yellow poplar. In the autumn, the leaves of deciduous trees change color and fall from the branches.

Indiana's deciduous trees are bare during the state's cold winter months.

Trees that require the same kind of soil and moisture grow side-by-side in the same forest. Softwood trees such as cypress and cottonwood grow in some of the state's wetlands, most notably in the southwest.

Some two hundred years ago, forests covered more than 85 percent of what is now Indiana. However, by 1922, the forests were so extensively cut that the state forester predicted that Indiana would one day have no forests at all. But that prediction proved to be wrong, thanks largely to government programs encouraging forest growth. Instead, over the past century, the number of acres with trees has increased. Today about 20 percent of the state has forests. Most of the trees are in the southern half of the state. William Hoover, a professor in the Department of Forestry and Natural Resources at Purdue University, has described the regrowth of the forests as "a tribute to the resiliency of nature."

People enjoy the beauty and seasonal changes of Indiana's forests. For many mammals, birds, and insects, the trees are needed for their survival. The forests are their habitat. Trees also help to clean the air and to prevent soil erosion. (If too much soil erodes, or wears away, the nutrients in the soil are lost, and plants and trees would not be able to grow roots and survive.) Trees are also valued as a building material.

The tallgrass prairie of the central United States and Canada extends into northwest Indiana. At one time, prairie covered about 15 percent of Indiana.

Quick Facts

HIGH AND BIG

The highest natural point in Indiana is the top of Hoosier Hill in Wayne County. It is 1,257 feet (383 m) above sea level. The lowest point, at 320 feet (98 m) above sea level, is in Posey County, where the Wabash River flows into the Ohio. The tallest building in the state is the Chase Tower in Indianapolis. With a height of 830 feet (253 m), it is the tallest building in the Midwest outside Chicago. Indiana's largest natural lake is Wawasee, in the northern part of the state. It has an area of more than 3,000 acres (1,200 ha). The largest artificial lake is Monroe, south of Bloomington. Its area is about 10,750 acres (4,350 ha).

Beautiful Lake Monroe, near Bloomington, attracts boaters on warm summer days.

The prairie has marshy areas as well as sparse stands of shrubs and oaks. Fire is necessary to the life cycle of the prairie. The fires keep the prairie open (with few or no trees) so grasses and wildflowers can have all the sunlight they need. Grasses and prairie plants survive the fires because they have deep, widespread roots. Even if the tops of the plants are burned, the roots are safe and able to send up new green growth after the fire has been put out.

Most of Indiana's prairie and wetlands have been lost to development of farms, roads, buildings, and other structures. But the soils, of course, remain and are now the base of some of Indiana's richest farmland.

Rivers and Water

Indiana has two main watersheds. (A watershed is a large area that is drained by rivers and other bodies of water.) One of the state's watersheds occupies a narrow strip across northern Indiana. Here, the rivers flow toward the Great Lakes. Their waters eventually reach the Saint Lawrence River, which continues to the Atlantic Ocean. The rivers of the other watershed flow toward the Ohio River or the Illinois River and then on to the Mississippi River and into the Gulf of Mexico.

The Saint Marys and the Saint Joseph rivers drain part of northeastern Indiana. They meet to form the Maumee River. The Maumee flows through Ohio and empties into Lake Erie. The city of Fort Wayne grew at this junction of the three rivers.

Another Saint Joseph River rises in southern Michigan, flows through extreme northern Indiana and returns to Michigan before emptying into Lake Michigan.

The industrial area in the northwest corner of Indiana is named the Calumet Region after the Grand Calumet and the Little Calumet rivers. These two slow-moving rivers empty into Lake Michigan. The rise of land separating them from the region draining into the Mississippi is called the Valparaiso moraine. It is a ridge of rubble left by one of the glaciers.

The Kankakee River crosses northwest Indiana and joins the Illinois River, which is a tributary of the Mississippi.

The Wabash River is the major river of Indiana. It rises in Ohio, flows

At Big Clifty Falls, Clifty Creek drops 60 feet (18 m) before flowing into the Ohio River.

west across Indiana, and then turns south. It forms the southern half of Indiana's western boundary and becomes increasingly twisty. The Wabash meets the Ohio River at the southwest corner of Indiana. Tributaries of the Wabash include Sugar Creek and the Mississinewa, Tippecanoe, and Eel rivers in the north and the Patoka and White rivers in the south. The White River has two long forks. In southern Indiana, sand dunes edge sections of the Wabash and White rivers.

The Whitewater River, near the state's southeastern boundary, flows into Ohio where it unites with the Miami River, a tributary of the Ohio River.

Falls of the Ohio State Park is on the north bank of the Ohio River in Clarksville, Indiana. Fossil beds along the shore contain the remains of creatures that lived in the region hundreds of millions of years ago, when it was part of a huge inland sea.

Indiana's water supply is drawn from groundwater (underground water) and from rivers and streams. Individuals, farms, industries, and state agencies work together to keep the water supply free of contamination.

The Seasons

Indiana has four distinct seasons. Winters are cold, with an average temperature near freezing. Snowstorms and ice are common, with the north of the state receiving more snow than the south. In spring, the days become longer and warmer. Summers are hot and humid. Day after day, the daytime temperature can stay in the 90s Fahrenheit (about 32–37 degrees Celsius). In the fall, the days grow shorter and cooler.

Indiana receives about 40 inches (100 cm) of precipitation each year. Most of this is in the form of rain. Thunderstorms can travel through Indiana, and tornadoes occasionally touch down, causing extensive damage to the landscape and buildings.

Wildlife

Some of the mammals living in Indiana include moles, shrews, chipmunks, squirrels, bats, woodchucks, and opossums. Beavers, once hunted for their fur, build their lodges in the state's ponds and streams. Foxes and bobcats are sometimes seen. Deer were plentiful in the early 1800s, but by a hundred years later, they had almost disappeared from the state—a result of hunting and loss of habitat, as more and more land was turned into farms or developed for other purposes. Authorities worked to rebuild and protect deer herds, and eventually deer became so numerous that the damage they caused to crops and trees became a growing problem. The number of motor vehicle accidents involving deer also increased. To keep the deer population in check, hunters using bows and arrows or guns are now allowed to hunt during certain times of the year.

Fish such as bass, catfish, pike, and sunfish are plentiful in Indiana's lakes and streams. They provide food for wild animals, but they also make fishing

A century ago, Indiana's deer population had dropped sharply because of hunting and loss of habitat, but deer are once again numerous in the state.

Eyeless cave fish live in underwater caverns where there is little or no light.

popular in the state's bodies of water. Darters—a kind of small fish that lives in streams—and eyeless cave fish are rare and are not allowed to be fished for sport.

Many birds pass through Indiana on their spring and fall migrations. Other birds are year-round residents. Ducks, geese, herons, and bitterns frequent the marshes and ponds. Meadowlarks, sparrows, warblers, orioles, wrens, blue jays, thrushes, woodpeckers, and flickers are common on the edges of fields and in wooded areas. Birds of prey, such as owls, hawks, and peregrine falcons, hunt small animals and other birds. Osprey and bald eagles are rare, though wildlife experts are working to increase these large birds' numbers.

Endangered Species in Indiana

Habitat loss is the main reason that plants and animals become rare or extinct (a type of plant or animal that is extinct has completely died out). In Indiana, the landscape has changed greatly since the early pioneer days. As a result, certain species are extinct or endangered (at risk of becoming extinct). In other instances, some species survive only in small areas.

The Karner blue butterfly is one of the endangered species of Indiana. The wings of this small and pretty butterfly are blue on top. The gray undersides have orange and black spots. The Karner blue lives in northern Indiana in grassy areas that have a scattering of oak trees. In summer, this butterfly flutters among the wildflowers in open sunny patches. The females lay eggs on wild lupine, the only plant the caterpillars of this species eat.

People are working to restore natural areas used by the Karner blue. They have thinned the trees in some areas to make room for prairie plants, and they have planted more lupine. Specialists also raise butterflies in captivity to make sure they have lupine on which to lay their eggs and to ensure that the caterpillars have lupine to eat. Student Ali DeVries wrote, "People should be honored to have this butterfly inhabit our state."

Efforts are under way to restore the habitat of the endangered Karner blue butterfly.

Indiana Bat

During the winter, Indiana bats hibernate in dense clusters in caves. Only a few caves in southern Indiana are suitable for these rare bats. In spring, Indiana bats migrate to wooded areas near streams and rivers. They find places under peeling bark to roost and to raise their young. At night, they feed on flying insects.

Fox Squirrel

Fox squirrels live in forests close to Indiana's prairie or near cleared land. They dart between the trees and up and down the trunks and branches. For a nest, they weave together twigs with the leaves on them or move into an old woodpecker nest. Fox squirrels eat acorns, hickory nuts, and beechnuts. They bury extras for use later. Those living close to farmland may feast on corn.

Robin

At sunrise, robins are among the first birds to start singing. They run across lawns and stop to look for earthworms. As fall approaches, they comb shrubs for berries. Most robins migrate south for the winter, but if there is enough food, some robins will stay all year in Indiana.

Hickory

There are several types of hickory trees growing throughout Indiana. Hickory trees produce hard-shelled nuts. Animals such as squirrels bury some of the nuts, and if the nuts are left in the ground, they eventually sprout. In autumn the leaves of the hickory turn yellow.

Big Bluestem Grass

Big bluestem grass is one of the grasses of the tallgrass prairie. The stems can grow as high as 6 feet (2 m) or more, and the narrow leaves can be about 2 feet (60 cm) long. In late fall and winter when there is frost, the leaves turn reddish bronze.

Box Turtle

Box turtles have high-domed shells, which can have different patterns on them. When threatened, these turtles pull their head, legs, and tail completely inside their shell. Box turtles live on the forest floor where it is cool and damp.

From the Beginning

People have been living in the area that became the state of Indiana for at least 12,000 years. The people who lived in this area between 8000 BCE and about 1000–750 BCE are of the Archaic tradition, a term that historians and scientists have used to describe the ancient people of that time. One sign of where they lived are huge piles of mussel shells left beside some of the region's streams during late portions of the Archaic period.

The next group to inhabit the area is referred to as the people of the Woodland tradition. They lived throughout the Mississippi and Ohio valleys from about 1000–750 BCE to about 900 CE. They built mounds of earth near their villages. The mounds were important in their ceremonies. Mounds State Park on the White River near Anderson has some of these mounds.

People of the Mississippian tradition, who lived in what is now Indiana from about 900 to 1650 CE, also built mounds. Angel Mounds, a large town that was

The location of the ancient town of Angel Mounds is now preserved as the Angel Mounds State Historic Site.

At the Alton Goin Historical Museum, visitors can see the kinds of horse-drawn carriages used in centuries past.

built during the Mississippian period near the place where the Ohio and Wabash rivers meet, was a center for government, religion, and trade for these people. Several smaller communities from the Mississippian period were clustered along the rivers close to Angel Mounds.

Modern American Indians

The Miami were among the American Indian groups living in the 1600s across the region that includes present-day Indiana. They lived along the Saint Joseph River and in the Wabash Valley. Their principal town, which was called Kekionga, was located where the Saint Joseph and Saint Marys rivers meet to form the Maumee River.

Two groups closely related to the Miami in language and culture were the Wea and the Piankashaw. Groups such as the Lenape (also called Delaware), Shawnee, and Potawatomi moved into what is now Indiana in the 1700s.

Europeans

French traders and missionaries—people who brought Christianity to new areas—came to what is now Indiana in the second half of the 1600s. They pressed west and south from Canada by way of the rivers and lakes. They were eager to discover if they could make money off the land and to meet and trade with the native people in the area. One early explorer was René-Robert Cavelier, sieur de La Salle. He explored Lake Michigan and the Saint Joseph and Kankakee

René-Robert Cavelier, sieur de La Salle, was one of the first Europeans to explore the region that includes present-day Indiana.

rivers during the fall of 1679 and the winter of 1680. He continued west to the Upper Mississippi River.

News that the land had abundant wildlife, especially beavers and other valuable fur-bearing animals, brought more explorers and traders to the region. Missionaries also came and settled near some American Indian villages.

To have some control over the fur trade in what is now Indiana, the French built three forts. The first was built in 1717 at Ouiatenon, the principal Wea settlement. Fort Miamis was built next to Kekionga in about 1722. The third fort was established on the lower Wabash River, in the area inhabited by the Piankashaw, in about 1732. Called Vincennes, this third fort grew into what is today the oldest town in Indiana.

Beginning in the late 1600s and during the 1700s, France and England (which became Great Britain in 1707) fought a series of wars with each other. The last of these wars—which in North America was called the French and Indian War—began in 1754. When the war ended in 1763, Great Britain had won. As a result, almost all the land that France had controlled in eastern North America, including what would become Indiana, passed from France to Britain.

That same year, Britain's King George III proclaimed that the land west of the Appalachian Mountains was to be reserved for American Indians. People in Britain's American colonies along the Eastern Seaboard wanted to move west and settle this land. But the British government wanted good relations with the region's Indians, in order to avoid expensive wars and to protect

In Their Own Words

We do hereby strictly forbid, on Pain of our Displeasure, all our loving Subjects from making any Purchases or Settlements whatever, or taking Possession of any of the Lands above reserved, without our especial leave and Licence for that Purpose first obtained.

—From King George III's 1763 proclamation setting aside lands for the Indians

the fur trade. Therefore, no whites were permitted to settle there, and traders needed a permit to do business in this area. Despite the proclamation, some American colonists did cross the Appalachians to settle in the Ohio and Wabash valleys.

A New Nation

By the 1770s, many people in Britain's American colonies wanted to be free of British rule. In 1775, fighting began between colonists and British troops, and in 1776, the thirteen colonies that would form the United States declared their independence from Britain. After years of hard fighting, the colonists won the American Revolution. Under the Treaty of Paris of 1783 officially ending the war, Great Britain recognized American independence, and it agreed to give to the new United States all British land east of the Mississippi River, south of what is now Canada, and north of Florida. In 1787, Congress passed the Northwest Ordinance, which established the Northwest Territory. It consisted of all U.S. land north of the Ohio River and east of the Mississippi River. Nearly twenty years later, the state of Indiana would be carved from this territory.

In 1800, Congress created the Indiana Territory out of the Northwest Territory. Its capital was at Vincennes. William Henry Harrison was appointed governor of the new territory. Harrison made treaties with American Indian groups. Under Harrison's treaties, the Indians gave up large amounts of land. Because of these and similar treaties made later, some Indian groups had to move to other areas within the region. Other Indian groups had to leave the region completely. Many Indians moved to land west of the Mississippi River.

At this 1810 meeting, which almost ended in violence, Tecumseh and William Henry Harrison argued over rights to traditional Indian lands in Indiana.

Tecumseh, a leader of the Shawnee people, rallied many American Indians to oppose the white people who were settling on the traditional land of American Indians. He said that this land belonged to all Indians and that individual Indian groups did not have the right to sell or grant land to the whites. His followers gathered at the junction of the Tippecanoe and Wabash rivers.

Governor Harrison did not like the idea that American Indians might be preparing for war against the white people. So on November 7, 1811, Harrison led an army against the Shawnee in what would be called the Battle of Tippecanoe. The Indians were defeated.

Tecumseh, however, worked to rebuild his forces. Meanwhile, the War

In Their Own Words

. . . the only way to stop this evil, is for all the red men to unite in claiming a common and equal right in the land as it was at first, and should be now—for it never was divided, but belongs to all. . . . Sell a country! Why not sell the air, the clouds and the great sea, as well as the earth? Did not the Great Spirit make them all for the use of his children?

—Tecumseh, in an 1810 letter to William Henry Harrison protesting whites' settling on Indian land

In Their Own Words

Every person, however poor, may with moderate industry become in a very short time a land holder; his substance increases from year to year, his barns are filled with abundant harvests; his cattle multiply. . . . Truly may it be said of that fortunate and highly favored country, "A paradise of pleasure is open'd in the wild."

—Attorney and landowner Rufus Easton, in an 1816 letter on the attractions of settling north of the Ohio River

of 1812 broke out between the United States and Britain. Tecumseh sided with the British. Harrison was named commander of the U.S. Army of the Northwest, and in 1813, he decisively defeated British and Indian forces in the Battle of the Thames in Canada. Tecumseh was killed in the battle. The war with Britain ended in 1815. Most Indians who remained in the Indiana Territory were soon forced out.

A New State

As more white settlers came to the Indiana Territory, it was divided into smaller units. The Michigan Territory was created in 1805, and then the Illinois Territory in 1809. The Indiana Territory's capital was moved to the town of Corydon in 1813. Indiana prepared to become a state. In the summer of 1816, delegates met to write a state constitution. On August 15 of that same year, Jonathan Jennings, who had been the territory's representative in Congress, was elected governor. A few months later, on December 11, 1816, Indiana became the nineteenth U.S. state.

After Indiana became a state, more and more people moved to the area. Many of these pioneers came to the state by way of the Ohio River. They came from Kentucky, Virginia, North Carolina, Pennsylvania, New York, and elsewhere. The Indiana constitution of 1816 barred slavery, but it did not clearly state whether existing slaves had to be freed. Some white settlers brought their slaves with them to Indiana.

The land these new arrivals entered was densely wooded. It could take years for a farm family to clear the land of all the trees and stumps. But once it was cleared, the land served the farmers well. As soon as a field was clear enough to be planted, corn, hay, potatoes, and flax were among the first crops to go in. Corn was a nutritious food, for both the family and its hogs. The extra corn was often made into whiskey. Fiber from the flax was woven into cloth. The trees that were cut down were used to build log cabins, fences, boats, and wagons. The wood was also burned for warmth.

One group of new settlers, the Rappites, was a religious group, originally from Germany, led by George Rapp. The Rappites came to Indiana in 1814. They wanted to create a harmonious, or peaceful, community. So they founded the town of Harmonie. They produced everything they needed and lived comfortably, until they moved to Pennsylvania in 1824. The following year, the town was sold to Robert Owen and William McClure. Owen planned it, now called New Harmony, as a model town in which everyone would be equal and all food and other supplies would be shared. But the people squabbled endlessly. Owen's experiment lasted for only two years.

The location of the Harmonie and New Harmony settlement is now a historic site where visitors can learn about life in the town in the nineteenth century.

MAKING POTPOURRI

To keep their homes, clothes, and blankets smelling sweet, settlers used a combination of dried flowers and herbs. Potpourri, as this fragrant mixture is called, is still used today. Follow these directions to create some homemade potpourri.

WHAT YOU NEED

Enough of the following to fill 4 or 5 cups (about a liter) total:

    flowers (such as roses, violets, or hollyhocks)
    herbs (such as lavender or rosemary)
    orange or lemon peel
    spices (such as cinnamon
        sticks or cloves)

Several sheets of newspaper

Spoon

2 or 3 covered jars

Collect the flowers and herbs. If you have access to a garden with the right plants, ask permission to pick some flowers or herbs. You may also go to a market or local nursery for these items.

Spread the newspaper in a warm, dry area where it can be left undisturbed for a few weeks. Place the flowers, herbs, and orange or lemon peel on the newspaper and leave them to dry out for about eight to ten days.

Once everything is dry, pick off the flower petals and herb leaves. Make separate piles of petals or leaves for each type of flower and herb.

Allow these to dry for another eight to ten days. Check on the leaves and petals every day to make sure they are drying out evenly.

When everything is dry, try combining the petals, leaves, orange or lemon peel, and spices in different proportions to create different scents. Using more cinnamon or cloves will produce a spicy aroma. Using more flower petals and lavender will create a sweet floral scent. Adding more orange or lemon peel to a mixture will change the scent a bit.

Pick the two or three scents you like the best, and spoon each combination of ingredients into a separate jar. Cover the jars and let them "age" for about two weeks. Be sure to shake the jars at least once a day so the ingredients are mixed. At the end of two weeks, your potpourri is ready to use.

You can put the potpourri in open dishes to make a room smell nice, or put it in little pouches to be placed in drawers or closets. The pouches make great gifts for family and friends.

Growth and Indian Removal

Abraham Lincoln's family was among the early settlers who came from Kentucky. Lincoln was seven years old when his father took the family across the Ohio River into Indiana. The Lincolns arrived in 1816 and stayed for fourteen years before moving to Illinois. Like many other Indiana families, the Lincolns lived on a large tract of land—about 160 acres (65 ha). But only a small portion of the land was cleared and farmed.

During early statehood, although most American Indians had already left the area, a few groups still remained in Indiana. However, treaties that were negotiated with the Wea, Miami, Lenape, and Potawatomi in 1818 took away more of their land or required them to move farther west. The Potawatomi were forced to leave in 1838, and the Miami finally surrendered the last parcel of tribal land in Indiana in 1846.

In 1820, the state legislature decided to build a new capital. The following year, it approved a recommendation that the capital be located at the center of the state. The lawmakers chose to call this place Indianapolis. The state government moved to Indianapolis in 1825.

Transportation and Internal Improvements

Transportation was of great concern to the new state. People wanted a dependable way to move goods to markets in the eastern and southern states. Building a network of roads, canals, and railroads seemed to be the answer. In 1826, the legislature decided to build a north-south highway through the state. This would be called the Michigan Road. The east-west National Road, a project begun by the federal government, was extended across Indiana in 1827–1834. It was used by wagons that carried people and goods between Maryland in the east and Illinois in the west. (The Michigan Road's route is now covered by several different highways. The National Road is now U.S. Highway 40.)

In 1836, the legislature passed the Mammoth Internal Improvements Act. The act provided $10 million to be used to build canals and rail lines and to improve the roads. Unfortunately, only small sections of the canals were built at that time. It would not be until 1853 that the Wabash and Erie Canal, which went from Lake Erie to Fort Wayne and then south to Evansville, would be completed. But by then, canals were not as useful as they might have been twenty years earlier. By the 1850s, railroads had become the preferred means of long-distance travel.

Slavery and the Civil War

Although slavery was officially barred in Indiana, many Indianans were not opposed to slavery. Many believed, for example, that there was nothing wrong with white people having slaves in the Southern states or even in the new territories and states being created farther west as the United States grew. The legislature passed laws that were meant to prevent or to at least discourage free blacks (African Americans who had never been slaves or had been legally freed from slavery) from settling in Indiana. Few Indianans believed that slavery should be abolished (ended) nationwide.

Nevertheless, the Underground Railroad did have routes through Indiana. This was not an actual railway. It was a network of people who helped and sheltered escaped slaves fleeing to states prohibiting slavery or to Canada or other countries. The journey was risky for the slaves and for their guides and protectors. The town of Newport (now called Fountain City) was a "station," or stopping place, on the Underground Railroad. Many escaped slaves found shelter there in the home of Levi and Catharine Coffin, who were Quakers.

Levi Coffin helped many slaves escape to freedom on the Underground Railroad.

HOOSIERS ARE WHO?

People who live in Indiana are called Hoosiers. The nickname was already popular in the 1830s when it began to appear in print. Many people have tried to explain the origin of the word. One idea is that it was brought to the region by settlers from areas of the South where people who lived in the hills used to be called "hoosiers," from an old English word for hill. Another theory suggests that Indiana river men were so good at beating, or "hushing," their opponents in fights that they became known as "hushers," which eventually became "hoosiers." Yet another theory is that a man called Hoosier used to hire workers from Indiana for the Louisville and Portland Canal, and these people came to be known as "Hoosier's men." These are only some of the explanations that have been proposed. None is completely convincing.

Meanwhile, in 1851, voters in Indiana approved a new state constitution. Article XIII of the constitution stated harsh rules regarding African Americans. It made it illegal for African Americans to come into or to settle in Indiana. It prohibited anyone from giving a job to an African American. In addition, any legal agreements made with African Americans would be considered worthless. In 1866, the Indiana supreme court declared Article XIII null and void, which means it was invalid. This article was officially repealed in 1881.

Even before the Civil War began in 1861, Indianans debated whether the Southern states should be permitted to secede, or separate, from the Union (another name commonly used for the United States at that time). In the months after Abraham Lincoln was elected president in November 1860, eleven Southern states did secede, forming the Confederate States of America. Lincoln was personally opposed to slavery, and many white Southerners believed the future of slavery in the United States was threatened by his election. Many Hoosiers sympathized with the Southern states. But Oliver Morton, who was governor in 1861–1867, believed the Union should be preserved. So during the Civil War, Indiana

INDIANA'S CIVIL WAR BATTLE

The Confederate side won the only Civil War battle that took place in Indiana. On July 8, 1863, some 2,500 Confederate cavalrymen under General John Hunt Morgan crossed the Ohio River into Indiana. The next day they moved on nearby Corydon, a former state capital. The Union force defending the town numbered just a few hundred men. It was easily defeated by the Confederates, who plundered the town and then headed northeast, eventually entering Ohio.

stayed in the Union, and it sent men to fight on the Union (or Northern) side. There was little actual fighting in the state during the Civil War. After four years of bloody fighting elsewhere, the South was defeated in 1865, the Southern states were returned to the Union, and the Thirteenth Amendment to the U.S. Constitution was adopted, abolishing slavery throughout the United States.

Leading to the Twentieth Century

By the 1860s, the landscape of Indiana was greatly changed from what it had been at the beginning of the century. About one-half of the forests had been cleared. Roads, railroads, and waterways made it easier for people to come to Indiana or for Indianans to travel to and ship goods to other states.

During this time, most Hoosiers still lived on farms, but small towns were growing. There were many new mills and factories using the resources of Indiana to manufacture a great variety of industrial and household products. With the end of the Civil War, immigration from the South to Indiana was renewed. The population, once concentrated in the southern half of the state, began to spread northward.

The Grange, a social and educational organization for farm families, came to Indiana in 1869. Grange members joined together and formed cooperatives. This allowed them to bargain for more favorable shipping rates for their farm products. The Grange also asked state legislators for better tax rates and to have mail delivered to addresses in rural areas.

By the late 1800s, Indiana had become a major manufacturing state. In this photo from the mid-twentieth century, workers make toys at a factory.

Laborers in Indiana's factories became active in labor unions. These organizations brought workers together so they could bargain with factory owners for better wages and working conditions. The Knights of Labor, a group that fought for workers' rights, gained many members in the early 1880s. It allowed women to be members and worked to get approval of an eight-hour workday, instead of the ten-hour or twelve-hour days that many people at that time were forced to work.

Natural gas was discovered in northern Indiana in 1867. Twenty years later, gas wells tapped this fuel so that it could be used. Many people thought the gas supply would last forever. Anyone who opened a factory could use the gas for free. This free gas led to Kokomo and Anderson being transformed into manufacturing towns. Muncie, called the City of Eternal Gas, was known for glassmaking and for steel, nail, and wire production. By the start of the twentieth century, however, the gas was pretty much used up, and the industrial boom fizzled out.

Quick Facts

MOTHER OF VICE PRESIDENTS

Indiana is sometimes called the Mother of Vice Presidents. Five men from Indiana have been elected vice president of the United States: Schuyler Colfax (under President Ulysses S. Grant), Thomas A. Hendricks (President Grover Cleveland), Charles W. Fairbanks (President Theodore Roosevelt), Thomas Marshall (President Woodrow Wilson), and Dan Quayle (President George H. W. Bush).

But progress continued in Indiana. For instance, Elwood Haynes test-drove a self-propelled, gasoline-powered vehicle on the roads outside Kokomo on July 4, 1894. Within a few years, Indiana had hundreds of companies building cars and making car parts. Studebaker, which had started in 1852 as a blacksmith shop and wagon-maker, began to make electric cars in 1902. Then, in 1904, the company started making gasoline-powered cars. Cars changed how people spent their leisure time. "We got to go to lots of things we couldn't go to if we didn't have a car," reported an Indiana woman in the 1920s. At the end of the nineteenth century, Indiana was a leading center for car manufacturing in the United States. Michigan came to dominate the automobile industry. But in 1909, Indiana still ranked second, producing about 13 percent of the country's automobiles, compared to Michigan's 51 percent.

In the late 1800s and early 1900s, the Calumet region, east of Chicago, developed into one of the nation's important industrial centers. The Standard Oil Company began building an enormous oil refinery at Whiting in 1889, to make gasoline and other products from crude oil. It went into operation the following year. Inland Steel started constructing a steel mill at East Chicago, Indiana, in 1901.

The Inland Steel Company began making steel in Indiana in the early 1900s.

Then, in 1905, the United States Steel Corporation bought 9,000 acres (3,600 ha) of land on the shore of Lake Michigan. It had plans to level the sand dunes and to build the world's largest steel mill. It would also build a town, to be named Gary. Rail lines and harbors already served the region, and numerous large and small mills and factories opened in the Calumet. People heard there were jobs to be had at U.S. Steel and other companies, and they came to Indiana to work. Many of them came from as far away as Eastern Europe, including Poles, Hungarians, Czechs, and Slovaks.

Challenging Times

Things were not always positive in the early part of the twentieth century. For instance, a branch of the Ku Klux Klan (also referred to as the KKK) was set up in Evansville, Indiana, in 1920. The KKK was an organization that was against African Americans and also Jews and Catholics. Membership in the Klan grew to 250,000 people in Indiana in the early 1920s. In the 1924 elections, the influence of the Klan helped the governor, a majority of state legislators, and several city mayors to win office. The power of the Klan in Indiana crumbled after its leader in the state, D. C. Stephenson, was convicted of murder in 1925. Some Klan activity continued, however, in subsequent decades.

KKK members hand out literature to passing motorists during a 1972 demonstration in Columbus.

Other problems came to Indiana beginning in the late 1920s. The Great Depression, which started in 1929, hit Indiana hard. During this time of severe economic hardship, prices for farm products dropped and factories closed or cut back on their operations. By 1933, about one-quarter of workers in the state were out of work. And in some towns, unemployment was much higher. In southern Indiana, the flooding of the Ohio River in 1937 added to the region's difficulties.

During this time, African Americans were faced with even more challenges. Indiana had separate schools for white and black students. Segregated schools remained legal in Indiana until 1949. This often meant that African-American children attended poorer schools that were not equipped with materials that white students had. Desegregation laws—which were designed to make things equal for African Americans and whites—went into effect, but some school districts disregarded them. It would take many more decades for some schools to arrange to have black and white students together.

New Growth

Life started to get a little better around the middle of the century. During World War II, Indiana's economy bounced back. Fighting had begun in Europe in 1939, and the United States entered the war in 1941. Farms and industries, especially steel, helped to supply the war effort. Then, after World War II ended in 1945, manufacturers turned their attention to making consumer goods. For instance, things such as refrigerators were made in Evansville. So many refrigerators were made there that Evansville for a while was known as the refrigerator capital.

During the 1950s, many people began to buy houses in the suburbs around Indiana's larger cities. Many small stores in the downtown areas of large cities closed their doors and moved to the new shopping malls, which were often located in the suburbs. This made the downtown areas of large cities look empty and worn out. Then, in the 1960s, to correct this problem, the federal government provided money and support for urban renewal projects. These projects helped cities such as Indianapolis and Gary to benefit from the creation of new housing and business districts, as well as civic, cultural, and recreational facilities.

In the following decades, Indiana weathered cycles of economic good times and bad times. Some businesses and industries failed while others flourished. Many people from across the country and around the world moved to the state. By 1999, Indiana's population rose past 6 million.

Meanwhile, natural disasters from time to time tested Indiana residents. A particularly deadly spate of tornadoes struck central and northern areas of the state on April 11, 1965. That day, which happened to be Palm Sunday, 137 people were killed as eleven tornadoes hit twenty counties. A record thirty-seven tornadoes tore through thirty-one counties on June 2, 1990. In June 2008, record flooding caused damage estimated at more than a billion dollars in central and southern areas of the state.

Through it all, residents of Indiana remained strong and continued to work toward making their state the best it could be. Toward the end of the 1990s, for example, Indianapolis's public facilities began to see one upgrade after another. A new arena for the city's pro basketball teams opened in 1999. This was followed by major expansions of the Indianapolis Museum of Art and the Eiteljorg Museum of American Indians and Western Art, a new billion-dollar international air terminal, a new retractable-roof stadium, and reconstruction of the Interstate 495 bypass on the west side of the city.

In the early twenty-first century, Indianapolis International Airport got a new state-of-the-art terminal building.

★ **10,000** BCE Ancient people live in the region that will include present-day Indiana.

★ **1100–1450** CE Angel Mounds is a site for early American Indian communities.

★ **1679** French explorer René-Robert Cavelier, sieur de La Salle and his party cross through the northwestern part of present-day Indiana.

★ **1732** Europeans establish their first permanent settlement—Vincennes—in what is now Indiana.

★ **1783** The American Revolution ends. Land that includes present-day Indiana becomes part of the United States.

★ **1787** The Northwest Territory is created.

★ **1800** The Indiana Territory is created.

★ **1816** On December 11, Indiana becomes the nineteenth state.

★ **1825** The state government meets in Indianapolis, the new capital.

★ **1836** The Mammoth Internal Improvements Act is passed to improve conditions in Indiana.

★ **1889** The Standard Oil Company builds an oil refinery at Whiting.

★ **1894** Elwood Haynes test drives an early automobile.

★ **1906** The United States Steel Corporation begins construction of a steel plant in the Calumet region.

★ **1911** The first Indianapolis 500 auto race takes place.

★ **1970** Orville Redenbacher starts his popcorn company in Indiana and calls it the Redbow Popcorn Company.

★ **1990** Indianapolis's Chase Tower, the tallest building in Indiana, opens.

★ **2006** For the first time since 1970, most Indiana counties begin observing Daylight Saving Time.

★ **2008** Indianapolis opens a new retractable-roof stadium, costing more than $700 million, for sports and concerts.

The People

The people of Indiana are a mix of long-time Hoosiers and newer residents. They represent the variety of histories and heritages that have come together in Indiana. Most people in Indiana belong to families who have lived in the state for more than a generation. About 68 percent of Indiana's people were born in the state, and nearly everyone—96 percent—was born in the United States. If they move, Hoosiers do not move far. They tend to move within the same county they have been living in or to a county close by.

Cities and Towns

Indiana has only a handful of midsized cities. Many Hoosiers live in small towns or in the suburbs around the bigger cities.

The population of Indiana today is concentrated in the middle and in the north of the state. Marion County, in the center of the state, has the highest population. It contains Indianapolis, the state's largest city and capital.

Lake County, in northern Indiana east of Chicago, is the second-largest county in

Quick Facts

CENTER OF THE UNITED STATES

Ever since the United States was formed, its population has grown, and more and more people have settled in its western areas. As a result, the center of population has moved west across the nation. But at one time, between 1890 and 1940, the center of population was in Indiana.

Hoosiers of all ages love basketball, including these fans enjoying an Indiana Fever game.

Notre Dame University is located just outside the city of South Bend.

terms of population. The city of Gary is in Lake County. Allen County, also in the north, is the third-largest county. Fort Wayne, the second-largest city in Indiana, is located in Allen County.

Evansville, in southern Indiana, is the third-largest city. Other sizable cities and towns are South Bend, Hammond, Bloomington, Fishers, Carmel, and Muncie. Many of Indiana's smaller towns have only a few hundred to a few thousand residents.

Racial Groups

In Indiana, more than 85 percent of the population is white. Many white people trace their roots to the settlers of English, Scottish, Irish, or German descent who came to Indiana at the end of the 1700s and in the 1800s. Poles, Czechs, Slovaks, Hungarians, Serbs, Croatians, Slovenes, and other Eastern Europeans, as well as Greeks and Italians, came to northern Indiana at the end of the 1800s and in the early 1900s to work in the region's steel mills and in other industries.

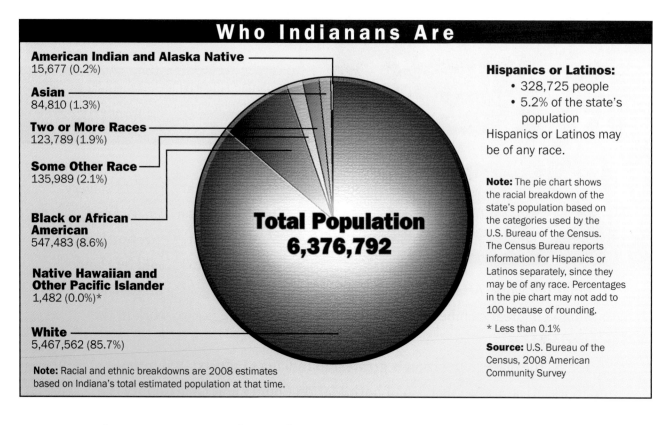

Who Indianans Are

American Indian and Alaska Native
15,677 (0.2%)

Asian
84,810 (1.3%)

Two or More Races
123,789 (1.9%)

Some Other Race
135,989 (2.1%)

Black or African American
547,483 (8.6%)

Native Hawaiian and Other Pacific Islander
1,482 (0.0%)*

White
5,467,562 (85.7%)

Total Population 6,376,792

Hispanics or Latinos:
- 328,725 people
- 5.2% of the state's population

Hispanics or Latinos may be of any race.

Note: The pie chart shows the racial breakdown of the state's population based on the categories used by the U.S. Bureau of the Census. The Census Bureau reports information for Hispanics or Latinos separately, since they may be of any race. Percentages in the pie chart may not add to 100 because of rounding.

* Less than 0.1%

Source: U.S. Bureau of the Census, 2008 American Community Survey

Note: Racial and ethnic breakdowns are 2008 estimates based on Indiana's total estimated population at that time.

African Americans make up almost 9 percent of the population in Indiana. Many African Americans in Indiana are descended from people who moved to the state from the South. During the first half of the 1800s, African Americans who came to Indiana included slaves, escaped slaves, and free blacks. Some African Americans started all-black farming communities. Greenville Settlement, founded in 1822, Cabin Creek, founded in 1825, and Beech, founded in 1829, were among the first of these settlements. Many of these communities have since disappeared, but Lyles Station, which was started in the late 1840s by freed slaves from Tennessee, still has families living there.

The town of Lyles Station was founded by African Americans in the 1840s.

Asian Americans in Indiana contribute to the cultural diversity that is part of life in the state today.

After the abolition of slavery in 1865, African Americans from the South came north into Indiana so they could buy land or find other work. After World War I, African Americans began again to head to Indiana in great numbers. Many went to the Calumet region to work in the industries there.

Today, the black population is greatest in Indiana's industrial counties and in its cities. The population of both Marion County and Lake County is about 26 percent African American. The city of Gary is roughly four-fifths African American.

Other races have low representation in Indiana. About one percent of the population is Asian American. Most Asian Americans live in the larger cities and in the university towns of West Lafayette and Bloomington. American Indians, Native Alaskans, Native Hawaiians, and other Pacific Islanders make up less than one percent of the population in Indiana.

Hispanics

When answering questions from the U.S. Census Bureau, people may identify themselves as being Hispanic or Latino. They or their families are from a Spanish-speaking nation or culture. People who are Hispanic or Latino

In Their Own Words

East Chicago was a great place to grow up. It was an extremely diverse community. Roy, Lou, and I were very much aware of our Mexican roots, but we also had a strong sense of being Americans.

—Dr. William M. Vega, whose father worked in the steel mills of East Chicago

may be of any race. In Indiana they make up about 5 percent of the population, a small proportion when compared to the fact that they make up about 15 percent of the entire U.S. population. The majority of Indiana's Hispanics trace their roots to Mexico. Other Hispanics in Indiana are from such places as Puerto Rico, Cuba, and Central America.

Many people from Mexico moved to the Calumet region of Indiana in the 1920s. Some found jobs with railroad companies. Others worked in the steel mills there.

In recent years, the Hispanic population in Indiana has grown rapidly. About 40 percent of the foreign-born immigrants who settle in Indiana are from Mexico. Many Mexicans who come to Indiana move there to join their families and to find jobs. Today, the greatest number of Hispanics live in Lake County and Elkhart County and in the city of Indianapolis.

A growing number of people in Indiana are Hispanic American.

The Lilly Family: Pharmacists and Business Leaders

Eli Lilly was born in 1838 in Maryland, and his family moved to Indiana in 1852. Lilly studied chemistry and the medicinal uses of plants and other substances. In 1876, he opened a factory in Indianapolis to manufacture and research prescription drugs. The company grew, and in 1881 it was incorporated as Eli Lilly and Company. Eli Lilly died in 1898. Later generations of the Lilly family continued to run the company, which is now one of the largest manufacturers in the world of medicinal drugs.

Madam C. J. Walker: Business Leader

Born Sarah Breedlove in Louisiana in 1867, Walker (her husband's name) invented a hair treatment for black women and built a company that made and distributed beauty products for African-American women. She established the company's headquarters in Indianapolis in 1910. Walker became the first self-made female millionaire in the United States, and her company ranked as the country's most successful black-owned business. Its Indianapolis building now houses a theater center. The building became a National Historic Landmark in 1991. Walker died in 1919.

Janet Guthrie: Race Car Driver

Janet Guthrie was born in 1938 in Iowa. But she made Indiana history in the 1970s. In 1977, she became the first woman to compete in the Indianapolis 500. A skilled race car driver, she also was the first woman to race in the Daytona 500, a famous auto race in Florida. Before racing at the Indy 500, Janet Guthrie had also been a pilot, a flight instructor, and an engineer.

David Letterman: TV Talk Show Host

David Letterman was born in 1947 in Indianapolis. After studying radio and television at Ball State University in Muncie, he began his TV career in Indianapolis. He worked as a weather reporter and news anchor and also hosted a children's show, a talk show, and a late-night movie show. He already showed signs of the quirky humor for which he would later become famous. In 1975, he moved to Los Angeles and worked as a comedy writer and performer. He got his own TV show, a morning program, in 1980. It lasted just a few months, but a couple of years later he began his long career as a late-night talk-show host.

Larry Bird: Basketball Player

Larry Bird was born in West Baden, Indiana, in 1956. He was a top-scoring player for his high school basketball team at French Lick and for his college team, Indiana State University. Bird joined the National Basketball Association's Boston Celtics in 1979 and played thirteen seasons with them. His outstanding play earned him many awards. Bird coached the NBA's Indiana Pacers from 1997 to 2000. In 2003, he became the team's president of basketball operations.

Michael Jackson: Singer, Songwriter, and Dancer

Michael Jackson was born in Gary in 1958. When he was five years old, he began performing with a family singing group that became known as the Jackson Five. He later branched out on his own and made such top-selling albums as *Thriller* and *Bad*, earning the nickname "The King of Pop." His music had a distinctive sound that borrowed from such styles as R&B, soul, disco, and pop. Jackson received numerous awards and has been called the most successful entertainer of all time. He died in 2009.

Population Changes

In general, the population of Indiana is gradually increasing. This growth is due mainly to what is called "natural increase," which means that there are more births than deaths. Also, new residents keep coming to Indiana from other states and other countries.

Despite the overall trend of a slowly increasing population, in some recent years there have been more people moving out of the state than people moving from elsewhere into Indiana. The people who move away are often young and college educated.

Indiana's business and education leaders worry about the effect this loss of skilled people has on Indiana's economy. They are working to create research

Purdue and other universities in Indiana have advanced laboratories for training future scientists.

centers and companies to make Indiana attractive to these talented young people as well as to other people who may want to come live in the state.

Indiana has excellent colleges and universities that prepare its students for jobs in science, high-technology industries, education, and other businesses and professions. Major public universities include Indiana University, which has its main campus in Bloomington; Indiana State University, located in Terre Haute; Purdue University, with its main campus in West Lafayette; and a large Indiana University–Purdue University joint campus in Indianapolis. Perhaps Indiana's best-known private university is Notre Dame, a Catholic institution located near South Bend. Founded in 1842, Notre Dame served only a handful of students in its early years. By the twenty-first century, its enrollment was close to 12,000 students, drawn from across the United States and dozens of other countries.

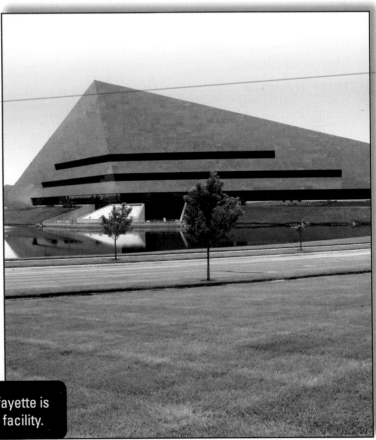

The MED Institute in West Lafayette is a high-tech medical research facility.

★ George Rogers Clark Day

During the American Revolution, George Rogers Clark led a Kentucky militia force across the Ohio River. He was determined to drive the British from the region north of the Ohio, so that Americans could safely settle and trade there. In Indiana, George Rogers Clark Day is observed on February 25, the day in 1779 when the British surrendered the fort at Vincennes to Clark.

★ March Madness: Hoosier Hysteria

March is a traditional time for basketball championship tournaments in the United States. The competition is exciting, and people talk about "March Madness." Indiana has its own version, known as Hoosier Hysteria. People in Indiana have a special passion for basketball, especially high school basketball. Competition among the boys' and girls' high school teams begins in the fall. In March, the teams with the most wins go to Indianapolis to play in the finals tournaments. The winners of the finals are the state champions.

★ Indianapolis 500

In the Indianapolis 500, thirty-three cars race two hundred times around the Indianapolis Motor Speedway to cover a total distance of 500 miles (804.7 km). They zip by the crowd at speeds of more than 200 miles (320 km) per hour. The Indy 500, as it is known, is held in Indianapolis on the last Sunday in May.

★ Bill Monroe Bluegrass Festival

Banjo players, fiddlers, and singers gather at Bean Blossom in June to share their love of bluegrass music. Bill Monroe, who is known as the father of bluegrass, founded the festival in 1967. It is the world's oldest continuously running annual festival devoted to bluegrass.

★ Madison Regatta

The town of Madison has seen plenty of river traffic pass on the Ohio. Around the Fourth of July, high-powered hydroplanes speed by in the Madison Regatta and the Governor's Cup race.

★ Three Rivers Festival

Fort Wayne, where three rivers meet, holds one of Indiana's largest summer festivals in mid-July. The festivities feature food, crafts, art, music, and contests, and the event concludes with a "fireworks finale."

★ Indiana State Fair

At the state fair, Indiana farmers show their best livestock and farm products, and manufacturers display the latest farm equipment and methods. Many people come for the rides and the entertainment, including concerts by big-name performers. The fair is held in August in Indianapolis. The first fair was held in 1852.

★ Grabill Country Fair

Grabill is located in an area where a large number of Amish people live. Many Amish people shun elements of modern technology, such as electricity and automobiles, and follow an older way of life. Traditional crafts and food draw people to Grabill in September, on the weekend after Labor Day. Music and contests for children and adults add to the festivities.

★ Riley Festival

The October birthday of Indiana poet James Whitcomb Riley is celebrated in Greenfield, which is Riley's birthplace. The Parade of Flowers, in which children leave flowers at the statue of Riley, is a tradition of the festival.

How the Government Works

Indiana has had two state constitutions. The first one was written in 1816, a little before Indiana became a state. The second constitution was written in 1851 and is the present-day constitution. It includes numerous changes, or amendments, that have been made over the years. The Indiana constitution begins with a bill of rights, which is a list of basic rights guaranteed to each person in the state. The constitution also describes the organization and powers of the state government.

Counties, Cities, Towns, and Townships

Indiana's ninety-two counties are made up of cities, towns, and townships. The state's legislature, also called the general assembly, decides how the county, city, town, and township governments are to be organized. These rules are spelled out in the Indiana Code—the set of state laws currently in effect. According to the code, counties, cities, towns, and townships are governed by a legislative branch and an executive branch. The counties, cities, towns, and townships have what is called home rule. This means that they may create rules and may form committees and agencies as needed. It allows them to conduct business in their areas for the good of their residents. The chief limitation on what they can do is that they cannot do things forbidden by the state constitution or by state law. Also, one government unit cannot use a power that is specifically granted to another unit.

The governor and legislature work in the Indiana Statehouse in Indianapolis.

In Indiana's counties (except Marion County), a three-member board of commissioners serves as the executive branch, and a seven-member county council works as the legislative body. Aside from Indianapolis, each city has a mayor as its executive and a common council as the legislative body. The legislative body in a town is the town council. The president of the town council is the town's executive. A township is led by a trustee and a township board. People are elected from their own county, city, town, or township to serve in these jobs.

The government of the city of Indianapolis and Marion County is different from that of the other cities in Indiana. In 1970, Indianapolis became what is called a consolidated city. The boundaries of Indianapolis were extended to match the boundaries of Marion County, where Indianapolis is located. In addition, the city and the county governments were combined to form a new government called Unigov. The legislative body is the city-county council. The mayor and the mayor's office form the executive branch. Although Unigov covers all of Marion County, a number of cities and towns in the county keep certain powers.

On the local level the state's public schools are managed by units of government called school districts or school corporations.

State Government

Like the federal government, the Indiana state government has three branches: the executive, legislative, and judicial. Each branch has its own powers and responsibilities. The executive branch is headed by the governor. The legislative branch is the lawmaking body. The judicial branch consists of the courts.

Indiana's schools are overseen by the state board of education. This board is headed by an elected official, the superintendent of public instruction. It has ten other members, who are appointed by the governor.

How a Bill Becomes a Law

Indiana's legislators create laws and programs to help their districts and the state. For example, they vote on the amount of money to spend on programs such as education, transportation, and public health.

Branches of Government

EXECUTIVE ★ ★ ★ ★ ★ ★ ★ ★

The executive branch enforces the laws of Indiana. The governor is Indiana's chief executive. The governor and lieutenant governor are elected together to serve for a term of four years. Other elected officials in the executive branch with four-year terms include the attorney general, secretary of state, auditor, treasurer, and superintendent of public instruction. The governor, lieutenant governor, secretary of state, auditor, and treasurer cannot serve more than eight years in any twelve-year period.

LEGISLATIVE ★ ★ ★ ★ ★ ★ ★ ★

The state legislature is known as the general assembly. It creates laws for the state. It has two houses, or chambers: the senate and the house of representatives. The senate has fifty members, and the house of representatives has one hundred members. Senators are elected to a four-year term, and representatives to a two-year term. There is no limit on the number of terms a member of the legislature may serve.

JUDICIAL ★ ★ ★ ★ ★ ★ ★ ★ ★

The supreme court is the highest court in Indiana. It has five judges, called justices. One of the five is the chief justice. The state also has a court of appeals with fifteen judges—three for each of the state's five districts. The supreme court and the court of appeal are appellate courts: they review the decisions made in the lower courts. Another appellate court is the tax court, which deals specifically with tax cases. Lower courts that conduct trials include the circuit courts and, in some counties, superior courts. There are also city and town courts in some counties. Appeals from city and town courts are heard in circuit and superior courts. In addition, Marion County has a small claims court, and St. Joseph County has a probate court, which deals with wills and related matters. Supreme court justices are picked by the governor from a list of candidates prepared by a special commission. After the governor's choice serves for two years, the people vote on whether to keep the person on the court for another ten years.

In the legislative process, a law begins as a bill, which is a proposal, or suggestion, for a law. To reach its final form, a bill goes through a series of steps. If a bill is to become a law, it must be kept alive all through the process. At any stage, if it does not advance to the next step, the bill may die.

Completed in 1888, the Indiana Statehouse took eight years to build.

Any senator or representative may introduce a bill. There's one exception: bills for raising money must originate in the house of representatives. Often the idea for a bill comes from state residents who send their ideas to their legislators. Once a bill is introduced, it next travels through its chamber of origin, either the senate or the house of representatives.

After the bill is introduced, it is scheduled for its first reading. At the first reading, the title is read aloud to the legislators in the chamber. Then the bill is assigned to a committee of legislators. The committee schedules a public hearing for the bill. People, organizations, and companies may come to the hearing to discuss the things they like and the things they do not like about the bill. After the hearing, the committee may vote on the bill or table it (take no action). If the committee tables the bill, it will die unless the committee votes on it later. If the committee votes on the bill and approves it by a majority vote of the committee members present, the bill advances.

If the bill advances, it is eligible for a second reading in the chamber. At the second reading, legislators may propose amendments, or changes, to the bill. For an amendment to be added, it must be approved by a majority of the legislators voting (a simple majority). Then the whole bill is voted on by the chamber. If it fails to win the approval of a simple majority, it dies. If the bill passes, it is now ready for the third reading.

If a third reading is scheduled, more amendments can be proposed. For these amendments to be added, they must be approved by a two-thirds majority of the legislators. This means that two-thirds of the legislators must vote in favor of the amendments. Then the whole bill is voted on again. If a "constitutional" majority of legislators (at least 26 members in the senate or 51 members in the house of representatives) votes in favor of the bill, then it will move on to the next chamber—either the senate or the house of representatives.

Quick Facts

INDIANANS IN CONGRESS

Indiana is represented in the U.S. Congress in Washington, D.C. Like all states, it has two members in the U.S. Senate. The number of members each state has in the U.S. House of Representatives is related to the state's population. Based on the results of the 2010 U.S. Census, Indiana has nine representatives in the U.S. House.

Governor Mitch Daniels delivers a speech to the state legislature.

In the second house, the bill goes through the same steps as it did in the first chamber. If the bill makes it through the second chamber with no changes, then it goes to the governor. But if the second chamber makes changes in the bill before approving it, then the bill is returned to the first chamber for consideration of these changes. The first chamber may agree to all the changes. If so, then the bill goes to the governor. If the first chamber does not accept all the changes, the bill is sent to a conference committee made up of two members from each chamber. The conference committee tries to come up with a compromise version of the bill. If both chambers approve the resulting compromise bill, it is finally sent to the governor.

When presented with a bill, the governor has three choices. He or she can sign the bill into law, veto it, or do nothing. If the governor takes no action for seven days, the bill will become a law anyway. If the governor vetoes, or rejects, the bill, the legislators can try to override the veto. A constitutional majority of both the senators and the representatives is required to override the governor's veto and to make the bill a law.

Getting Involved

It is a good idea for voters to stay informed so they can understand the different sides of issues and can pick candidates who share their ideas and principles. To be informed, voters listen to television and radio reports, read newspapers (either in print or online) and visit the websites of news organizations, and talk with their neighbors. Many people attend public meetings of the state and local governments. Hoosiers contribute to the decision-making process in their state by writing to their legislators and speaking at hearings. They organize campaigns and volunteer their time to create interest and support for their favorite issues or candidates. Students who are curious about the workings of the general assembly can serve as a senate page for a day.

Making a Living

Indiana has a reputation for being an agricultural state, and people working in agriculture make a significant contribution to the economy. But other activities contribute to the state economy as well. People work in manufacturing, service jobs, transportation, and mining. In Indiana, the proportion of the workforce working in manufacturing is greater than in any other state.

Agriculture Today

Farms are found throughout Indiana. Even urban counties, such as Marion and Lake counties, have some farmland. The soil, rainfall, and hot summers of Indiana make its farmland very productive.

Of all the agricultural products, corn brings in the most income. Soybeans are second, and hogs are third. Much of the corn, soybean, and oat harvests are used as animal feed for Indiana's hogs and other livestock. Corn is also sold as fresh ears, and some is packaged as popcorn.

"Indiana has the best tomatoes," claims one Hoosier. Indiana grows tomatoes for eating fresh and for processing. Cantaloupes and watermelons grow in the sandy soil of southwestern Indiana. Winter wheat, potatoes, hay, cucumbers for pickles, green beans, and onions are also important crops. Apples, peaches, and blueberries are grown as well.

A farmhouse looks out on a harvested cornfield. Corn is Indiana's leading crop.

Wind turbines, such as these standing in a soybean field, provide clean energy—and give some farmers another source of income besides their crops.

Poultry farms raise chickens, ducks, and turkeys. Some poultry farms specialize in egg and baby chick production. Ice cream is a leading dairy product. Indiana's meatpacking industry processes hogs, cattle, sheep, and poultry.

RECIPE FOR MINT-CHOCOLATE BROWNIES

Mint is an important Indiana product. By following this recipe, you can make a batch of brownies with a refreshing minty flavor.

WHAT YOU NEED

vegetable oil

$^3/_4$ cup (170 grams) butter

3 eggs

1 $^1/_2$ cups (300 g) sugar

1 teaspoon (5 milliliters) vanilla

$^1/_2$ teaspoon (2.5 ml) mint flavoring

$^1/_2$ cup (60 g) cocoa powder

$^3/_4$ cup (75 g) all-purpose flour

$^1/_2$ teaspoon (2 g) baking powder

salt

Have an adult help you with the oven. Preheat the oven to 350 °F (175 °C). Grease a brownie pan with a little bit of vegetable oil and set the pan to the side.

Put the butter in a mixing bowl and beat it until it is fluffy. Add the eggs, sugar, vanilla, and mint flavoring. Mix all the ingredients very well.

Add the cocoa powder, flour, baking powder, and just a pinch of salt and continue mixing until the batter is smooth. Carefully pour the batter into the pan.

Place the pan in the middle rack in the oven. Bake your brownies for about 30 minutes. To check whether they are done, carefully stick a knife or a toothpick into the center of the pan. If the brownies are done, the knife or toothpick will come out clean. Ask an adult to help you with this.

When the brownies are done baking, carefully take them out of the oven and set them aside to cool. When they are cool, you can cut them into small squares. Serve the brownies plain or with a little bit of ice cream or whipped cream.

Manufacturing

Indiana's factories make and process a wide range of products. The Calumet region of northwest Indiana is known for the production of high-quality steel. To make the steel, ingredients such as iron, coke, and limestone are heated in blast furnaces. The coke is made in the Calumet region, too. It is made from coal that is baked until it is almost pure carbon. At mini-mills, scrap steel is melted so that it can be reused. Steel beams, household and medical appliances, machinery, cans, and motor vehicles and parts are only a few of the things made of steel.

Indiana is a leader in the production of auto parts. Its factories turn out brakes, axles, pistons, exhaust pipes, carburetors, lighting, and electrical components for cars and trucks. There are also companies that make diesel engines for buses and heavy-duty construction equipment. Some plants make

There are many steel mills in northwestern Indiana, including this one in Portage.

Workers & Industries

Industry	Number of People Working in That Industry	Percentage of All Workers Who Are Working in That Industry
Education and health care	676,642	21.9%
Manufacturing	584,689	18.9%
Wholesale and retail businesses	436,906	14.1%
Publishing, media, entertainment, hotels, and restaurants	327,554	10.6%
Professionals, scientists, and managers	245,775	8.0%
Construction	199,362	6.5%
Banking and finance, insurance, and real estate	170,382	5.5%
Transportation and public utilities	156,963	5.1%
Other services	142,256	4.6%
Government	107,009	3.5%
Farming, fishing, forestry, and mining	43,097	1.4%
Totals	**3,090,635**	**100%**

Notes: Figures above do not include people in the armed forces. "Professionals" includes people such as doctors and lawyers. Percentages may not add to 100 because of rounding.

Source: U.S. Bureau of the Census, 2008 estimates

the bodies for delivery vans, trucks, ambulances, and shuttle buses. Other plants assemble cars and trucks. Campers, RVs, and motor homes are a specialty in Indiana's motor vehicle industry.

Major pharmaceutical companies have production plants and laboratories in Indiana. They research new drugs and treatments for both humans and animals and make pills and other medicines. The pharmaceutical company Eli Lilly and Company is one of the largest employers in Indiana. The company has a history of medical breakthroughs. It was the first to sell insulin as a treatment for diabetes, and it has developed many other important drugs.

Indiana's forests supply the forest products and hardwood industries. Loggers harvest the trees, and at sawmills the logs are cut into boards. The wood is used

Lumber from Indiana's forest products industry is used to build many homes.

in house construction and to make furniture. Trees such as oak, maple, cherry, and walnut are cut into thin layers of veneer. Veneer is used to cover furniture to give it beauty. Pulp made from scraps and odd pieces of wood is turned into paper products. Each step of the manufacturing process adds value to the wood and creates jobs.

Unfortunately, in recent years, a number of Indiana factories have closed. In many cases, the factories were important employers in their communities, and factory shutdowns can cause severe hardship for the people who once worked in those plants.

When the Whirlpool Corporation closed its refrigerator factory in Evansville in 2010, more than one thousand people lost their jobs. When such a closing happens, many workers either move to other cities and states in search of jobs or have to learn a new trade. Some workers have difficulty finding a new job that pays as well as the one they lost.

In Their Own Words

A lot of emotions out there, a lot of people just trying to figure out where their life goes from here.

—Evansville labor leader Darrell Collins, describing what it was like as the Whirlpool plant got ready to shut down production

Mining

Limestone may be the most widely known mineral that is mined in Indiana. The light gray or light tan stone covers many important buildings in the state and in the nation. Limestone is also carved into statues and into building elements such as columns and decorative molding. Limestone is cut from quarries located in south-central Indiana.

Another material mined in Indiana is coal. It is taken mostly from strip mines in the southwestern part of the state. Sand, gravel, clay, and shale are also widely collected. Limestone, sand, shale, and iron oxide are combined to make cement. Indiana also produces small amounts of oil and natural gas.

Mint

Peppermint and spearmint are grown in northwestern Indiana for their flavorful oil. In summer, the tops of the leafy plants are harvested, and the oil is distilled from them. Peppermint and spearmint oils are added to chewing gum, toothpaste, mouthwash, candy, and medicines.

Band Instruments

Trumpets, trombones, flutes, piccolos, clarinets, oboes, bassoons, saxophones, tubas, and sousaphones are among the band instruments manufactured in Indiana. Skilled musicians as well as beginners play these brass and woodwind instruments.

Furniture and Cabinets

Indiana is a top producer of wood office furniture and kitchen cabinets. Wood from oak, maple, tulip, ash, hickory, and cherry trees are favorite choices. These beautiful woods come from the forests of Indiana and neighboring states.

Orthopedic Implants

Artificial knees, hips, shoulders, elbows, and ankles are designed to replace diseased or damaged joints in people. Warsaw, Indiana, is a world center for the manufacturing of such orthopedic implants.

Recreational Vehicles

Many campers, trailers, motor homes, and recreational vehicles (RVs) are made in Indiana. Some manufacturers build the shell of these vehicles, while others craft and install all the interior details.

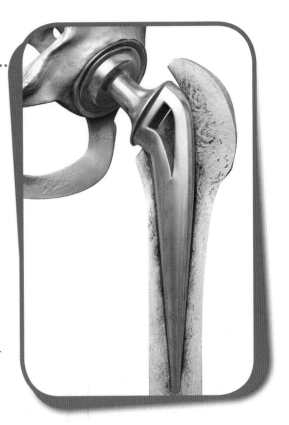

Soybeans

Soybeans grown in Indiana are used to feed the state's hogs and other livestock. The nutritious beans and soybean oil are also added to many food products sold in grocery stores. Soybean oil has nonfood uses, too. It is made into ink, crayons, and candles. Biodiesel fuel—which contains soybean oil—powers trucks, tractors, and buses.

Transportation

Highways, railroads, airports, and ports for ships all help Indiana's farmers and manufacturers to reach their customers. These passageways connect Indiana's cities and towns with Chicago, Illinois, and Louisville, Kentucky, as well as with more-distant transportation hubs throughout the nation. Trucks travel the interstate highways that run east-west across northern, central, and southern Indiana and north-south through Indianapolis. Railroads converge on Indianapolis, too. Indiana has three major ports. Two are on the Ohio River, at Mount Vernon and Jeffersonville. One is on Lake Michigan, at Burns Harbor in Portage. These ports handle large shipments of grain, coal, steel, and fertilizer. Many ships leaving these ports travel all the way to the Atlantic Ocean or the Gulf of Mexico. The Lake Michigan port handles the most oceangoing cargo of any U.S. port on the Great Lakes.

Construction workers complete a new barrier for an interstate highway.

Highways help people get to and from work and relaxing recreation areas. They also attract businesses and jobs to the areas they pass through. A number of high-technology companies are situated along Interstate 65, near West Lafayette and Purdue University, and along Interstate 69 in northeastern Indiana. Plans are under way to extend Interstate 69 from Indianapolis to Evansville in the southwest. Near Evansville, the new highway will use an existing road, Interstate 164, which extends about 21 miles (34 km) north of town. People hope that the new highway will draw businesses and new residents to southern Indiana and give the state economy a boost.

Service Jobs

Service jobs involve practicing a special skill or helping another individual or business. Service workers, for example, provide medical or dental care, business management, and legal advice. They perform jobs such as sales, computer programming, and accounting. They make car repairs and do cleaning. In Indiana, health-care workers, businesspeople, office workers, and food-service workers are among the most numerous types of service workers.

Other service workers include the state's many counselors, teachers, and scientists. Scientists usually have jobs in government agencies, companies, or colleges or universities. Teachers generally work in private or public schools or in colleges or universities.

Tourism

Tourism is another key service industry. The people who work in hotels, restaurants, and stores that tourists visit are service workers. So are workers such as museum staff members and tour guides.

Indiana has many tourist attractions. Some are part of the National Park Service—such as the Indiana Dunes National Lakeshore on Lake Michigan, the George Rogers Clark National Historical Park at Vincennes, and the Lincoln Boyhood National Memorial at Lincoln City. The Hoosier National Forest in south-central Indiana has interesting caves and karst features. There also are

The historic Bartholomew County Courthouse in Columbus was built in the 1870s. Next to it is a veterans memorial, honoring soldiers who fought in wars in the twentieth century.

three national wildlife refuges and dozens of state parks and forests located throughout Indiana.

Indianapolis's children's museum is the biggest in the world. The city is also home to other major museums, including the Indianapolis Museum of Art, the Eiteljorg Museum of American Indians and Western Art, the Indiana State Museum, and the Benjamin Harrison Presidential Site. (Harrison, who served as president of the United States from 1889 to 1893, was a longtime resident of Indianapolis.)

Indiana's many history-related attractions include the Conner Prairie Interactive History Park. Located in Fishers, near Indianapolis, it offers an outdoor re-creation of nineteenth-century life. The Indianapolis Symphony Orchestra plays at the park in the summer. Aviation pioneer Wilbur Wright was born in Indiana in 1867. His restored birthplace home, which is near Hagerstown, is now a museum.

Because of the state's long association with the automobile industry, there are many museums that attract car and racing buffs, such as the Auburn Cord Duesenberg Automobile Museum in Auburn, the Studebaker National Museum in South

FOOTBALL, TOO

When it comes to sports, Indiana is probably best known for auto racing and basketball. But football is also big. Notre Dame long ranked as one of college football's powerhouses. In recent years, Indiana has acquired an association with good quarterbacking. The Indianapolis Colts' Peyton Manning is one of pro football's superstars. Drew Brees, who led the New Orleans Saints to victory in the 2010 Super Bowl, played his college ball at Purdue.

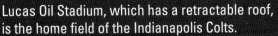

Lucas Oil Stadium, which has a retractable roof, is the home field of the Indianapolis Colts.

The Indianapolis 500 is one of the world's most famous auto races.

Bend, and the Hall of Fame Museum at the Indianapolis Motor Speedway.

The Speedway itself is one of the state's greatest attractions. But car racing is only one of the favorite sports pastimes of both Indianans and visitors to the state. Basketball and football are also popular. The state's professional teams include the Pacers in the NBA, the Fever in the Women's National Basketball Association, and the Colts in the National Football League. All three are based in Indianapolis. Fans of sports history flock to museums such as the Indiana Basketball Hall of Fame at New Castle and the College Football Hall of Fame in South Bend.

Working Together

The people of Indiana have used the resources of their state to make it a leader in agriculture and in manufacturing. They continue to invent products that are used throughout the nation and the world. People who work in transportation try new ways to move goods through the state as quickly and efficiently as possible. They help Indiana to send its products to faraway places. More and more, scientists and businesspeople in Indiana work together. They combine their ideas and knowledge to develop new ways to create products that will improve health care and agriculture. The energy and creativity of the people of Indiana have helped to make their state a good place to work and to live.

The torch at the center of the Indiana flag stands for liberty and enlightenment. The rays coming from the flame represent their far-reaching effect. Thirteen stars are arranged in a circle around the torch. They represent the original thirteen states. The five stars arranged in a half-circle represent the next five states to be admitted to the Union. The large star above the torch represents the nineteenth state, Indiana.

The state seal is in the shape of a circle. An outer circular band bears the words "Seal of the State of Indiana" and the date 1816 (the year that Indiana became a state). The small design on each side of the date includes a diamond and two leaves of the tulip tree, the state tree. The inner circle has two sycamore trees at the right. A man raises an ax to swing at the trees. On the left, a buffalo jumps over a log and into green grass. In the background, the sun shines above three hills.

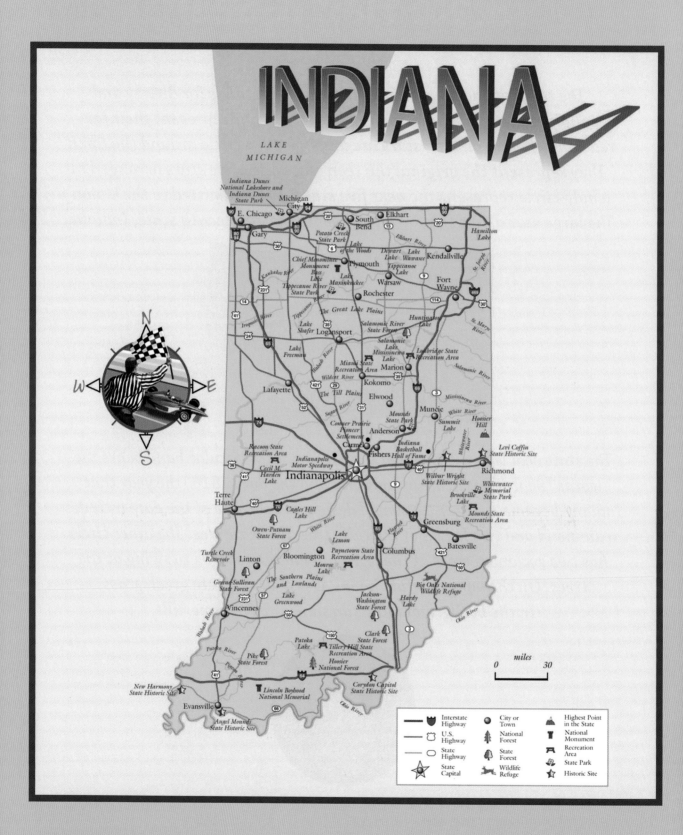

INDIANA

LAKE MICHIGAN

Indiana Dunes National Lakeshore and Indiana Dunes State Park

Michigan City

E. Chicago

Gary

South Bend

Elkhart

Hamilton Lake

Potato Creek State Park

Lake of the Woods

Elkhart River

Chief Menominee Monument

Bass Lake

Dewart Lake

Lake Wawasee

Kendallville

St. Joseph River

Kankakee River

Plymouth

Lake Maxinkuckee

Tippecanoe Lake

Tippecanoe River State Park

Warsaw

Fort Wayne

Rochester

The Great Lake Plains

Iroquois River

Tippecanoe River

Lake Shafer

Logansport

Salamonie River State Forest

Huntington Lake

St. Marys River

Lake Freeman

Salamonie Lake

Mississinewa Lake

Loudridge State Recreation Area

Salamonie River

Wabash River

Miami State Recreation Area

Marion

Lafayette

Wildcat River

Kokomo

The Till Plains

Elwood

Muncie

Mississinewa River

White River

Hoosier Hill

Mounds State Park

Summit Lake

Conner Prairie Pioneer Settlement

Anderson

Carmel

Raccoon State Recreation Area

Indianapolis Motor Speedway

Fishers

Indiana Basketball Hall of Fame

Levi Coffin State Historic Site

Cecil M. Harden Lake

Indianapolis

Whitewater River

Richmond

Wilbur Wright State Historic Site

Terre Haute

Cagles Mill Lake

White River

Brookville Lake

Whitewater Memorial State Park

Owen-Putnam State Forest

Lake Lemon

Paynetown State Recreation Area

Columbus

Mounds State Recreation Area

Greensburg

Batesville

Turtle Creek Reservoir

Linton

Bloomington

Monroe Lake

Flatrock River

Greene-Sullivan State Forest

The Southern Plains and Lowlands

Big Oaks National Wildlife Refuge

Lake Greenwood

Jackson-Washington State Forest

Hardy Lake

Vincennes

Wabash River

Clark State Forest

Patoka Lake

Tillery Hill State Recreation Area

Hoosier National Forest

Corydon Capitol State Historic Site

Pike State Forest

Patoka River

Pigeon River

New Harmony State Historic Site

Lincoln Boyhood National Memorial

Ohio River

Evansville

Angel Mounds State Historic Site

miles
0   30

Legend

Symbol	Description
	Interstate Highway
	U.S. Highway
	State Highway
	State Capital
	City or Town
	National Forest
	State Forest
	Wildlife Refuge
	Highest Point in the State
	National Monument
	Recreation Area
	State Park
	Historic Site

On the Banks of the Wabash, Far Away

words and music by Paul Dresser

BOOKS

Clark, Richard W. *Indianapolis, Indiana: A Photographic Portrait*. Rockport, MA: Twin Lights, 2007.

Conn, Earl L. *My Indiana: 101 Places to See*. Indianapolis, IN: Indiana Historical Society Press, 2006.

Finch, Jackie Sheckler. *It Happened in Indiana: Remarkable Events That Shaped History*. Guilford, CT: Globe Pequot Press, 2011.

Ling, Bettina. *Indiana*. New York: Children's Press, 2009.

Thomas, Phyllis. *Indiana off the Beaten Path, 9th edition*. Guilford, CT: Insiders' Guide, 2007.

WEBSITES

George Rogers Clark National Historical Park
http://www.nps.gov/gero

Indiana County History Preservation Society
http://www.countyhistory.com

Indiana Department of Natural Resources—Hey Kids!
http://www.in.gov/dnr/kids

Indiana Dunes National Lakeshore
http://www.nps.gov/indu

IN.gov—the Official State Website
http://www.in.gov

Indiana's Official Website for Tourism
http://www.in.gov/visitindiana

Lincoln Boyhood National Memorial
http://www.nps.gov/libo

Kathleen Derzipilski is a research editor who specializes in children's nonfiction. She lives in San Diego, California.

Richard Hantula is a writer and editor who lives in New York City.

Page numbers in **boldface** are illustrations.

African Americans, 26, 31, 32, 36, **36**, 37, **43**, 43–44, 46, 47
American Indians, **21**, 21–22, 23, 24–26, **25**, 30, **43**
American Revolution, 24
Anderson, 21, 34
animals, 4, **4**, 11, **15**, 15–16, **16**, **18**, 18–19, **19**
    endangered, 16–17, **17**
architecture, 5, 38, **38**, **56**, 72, **72**
area, 7
Asian Americans, **43**, 44, **44**
astronauts, 49
automobile industry, 35, 64, 66, 73–74
automobile racing, 39, 46, **46**, 50, 74, **74**

battles, 25, 26, 33
beaches. *See* dunes
Bird, Larry, 47
birds, 16, 18
    state bird, 4, **4**
borders, 7

Calumet region, 13, 35–36, 44, 45, 64, **64**
canals, 30–31
capital, 24, 26, 30
    See also Indianapolis
caves, 10, **10**, 16, 18, 71
children's museum, 72
Civil War, 32–33
Clark, George Rogers, 50, 71
climate, 14
constitution, state, 26, 32, 53
Coffin, Levi, 31, **31**
Corydon, 26
counties, 7, **9**, 41–42, 44, 45, 53–54, **72**
courts, 54, 55

dunes, 8, **8**, 13, 36, 71

East Chicago, 35, 44
economy, 30–31, 33–36, **34**, **35**, 37–38, 44–45, **48**, 48–49, **49**, **60**, 61–62, **62**, **64**, 64–71, **65**, **66**, **68**, **69**, **70**
education, 37, **42**, **48**, 48–49, 54, **65**, 71
endangered species, 16–17, **17**
ethnic and racial groups, 42–45, **43**, **44**, **45**
Evansville, 31, 36, 37, 42, 67, 71
executive branch, 54, 55, **58**, 59
explorers, **22**, 22–23

farming, 12, 14, 26–27, **27**, 33, 37, 43, **43**, 51, **51**, **60**, 61–62, **62**, **65**, 68, **68**, 69, **69**
festivals and events, **50**, 50–51, **51**
fires, prairie, 12
fish, 15–16, **16**
flag, state, 75, **75**
floods, 38
flower, state, 4
forests, **10**, 10–11, 18, **18**, 19, **19**, 33, **65**, **66**, 66–67, 68, 71–72
    state tree, 4, **4**
Fort Wayne, 12, 31, 42, 51
forts, 23
fossils, 5, **14**
France, 5, **22**, 22–23

Gary, 36, 37, 42, 44, 47
George III, King, 23
government
    federal, Indiana in, 34, 57
    of Indiana, 24, 26, 32, **52**, 54–59, **56**, **58**
    local level, 53–54, 59

Grange, 33
Great Depression, 37
Guthrie, Janet, 46, **46**

Harrison, Benjamin, 72
Harrison, William Henry, 24–26, **25**
Haynes, Elwood, 35
highest point, 11
Hispanic Americans, **43**, 44–45, **45**
historic sites, **21**, **27**, 43, **43**, **72**, 72–73
Hoosier Hysteria, 50, **50**
hunting, 15
hydroplanes, 51

Indiana Dunes National Lakeshore, 8, 71
Indianapolis, 30, 37, 38, **38**, 39, 41, 45, 46, 47, 49, 50, **52**, 54, 70–71, 72, 73, **73**, 74, **74**

Jackson, Michael, 47, **47**
Jennings, Jonathan, 26
jobs. *See* economy
judicial branch, 54, 55

karst, 10, 71
Ku Klux Klan (KKK), 36, **36**

labor unions, 34
lakes, 7, 8, **8**, **12**, 12–13, 15, 22, 31, 36, 70, 71
language, state, 5, **5**
La Salle, René-Robert Cavelier, sieur de, **22**, 22–23, 39
Latinos. *See* Hispanic Americans
legislative branch, 30–31, 32, **52**, 54–59, **56**, **58**
Letterman, David, 47, **47**
Lilly, Eli, 46, 66
Lincoln, Abraham, 30, 32, 71

Mammoth Internal
    Improvements Act,
    30–31
manufacturing. *See* economy
maps, **6**, **9**, **76**
McClure, William, 27
MED Institute, **49**
mining, 5, 65, 67
Morgan, John Hunt, 33
Mound Builders, **21**, 21–22
Muncie, 34, 42, 47
museums, **20**, 38, 71, 72–74
music, 47, **47**, 50, 51, 68
    state song, 77

name of state, origin, 24
Native Americans. *See*
    American Indians
natural gas, 34
natural resources, 5, 10–11,
    12–14, 26–27, 34, 61,
    65, 67
nickname, state, 5, 32
Northwest Territory, 24
Notre Dame University,
    42, 49, 73

Owen, Robert, 27

plants, 10–12, 19
    state flower, 4
    state tree, 4, **4**
population, 5, 38, 41–45,
    43, 48–49
ports, 70
prairie, 11–12, 19
project
    potpourri, 28–29
Purdue University, **48**, 49

Rapp, George, 27
recipe, 63
Redenbacher, Orville, 39
Riley, James Whitcomb, 51
rivers, 12–14, **13**, **14**, 22,
    23, 25, 70
    state river, 5
roads, 30, 38, **70**, 70–71

sand dunes. *See* dunes
seal, state, 75, **75**
seasons, 10, **10**, 14, 16, 18, 19
settlers, 23–24, 26–27, **27**,
    42, 43, **43**
size. *See* area
slavery, 26, 31–33, 43, **43**
song, state 77

South Bend, 42, 49, 74
sports, 38, 39, **40**, 47, 50, **50**,
    73, **73**, 74, **74**
springs, 10
statehood, 5, 26, 39, 75
stone, state, 5

Tecumseh, **25**, 25–26
till, 8
timeline, 39
Tippecanoe, Battle of, 25
tornadoes, 38
tourism, 71–74
transportation, 5, **20**, 30–31,
    38, **38**, **65**, **70**, 70–71, 73
trees. *See* forests

Unigov, 54

Valparaiso moraine, 13
Vincennes, 23, 24, 50, 71

Walker, Madam C. J., 46
watersheds, 12–13
    See also rivers
weather, 14, 38
websites, 59, 78
World War II, 37